6 Things

We Should Know About God

Leader Guide

6 Decisions
That Will Change Your Life

Participant Workbook
DVD
Leader Guide

6 Things
We Should Know About God

Participant Workbook
DVD
Leader Guide

6 Ways
We Encounter God

Participant Workbook
DVD
Leader Guide

6 Things

We Should Know About God

Leader Guide

Tom Berlin

with Karen Berlin

Abingdon Press
Nashville

Six Things We Should Know About God
Leader Guide

Tom Berlin with Karen Berlin

This book is printed on acid-free, elemental chlorine-free paper.

ISBN 978-1-426-79458-2

14 15 16 17 18 19 20 21 22 23—10 9 8 7 6 5 4 3 2 1
MANUFACTURED IN THE UNITED STATES OF AMERICA

Table of Contents

Introduction

Six Things We Should Know About God is a six-week small group experience that gives participants an opportunity to learn about different qualities of God's character and discuss the ways they are encountering God in their daily lives. The group will meet weekly to watch a video and complete Scripture study that will describe aspects of God's holiness, providing new perspectives into the character of God. The common goal of the Participant Workbook, DVD, and this Leader Guide is to provide an opportunity to look closely at the character of God and gain fresh insights into the character that God wants to form in each of us.

Covenant Formation

It is important that each group function out of a set of shared values. Coming to a consensus or a "covenant" about what group members can anticipate from their small group will help set a tone of trust and mutuality. It is important that each member knows the small group is a safe environment to share personal information. You are encouraged to make confidentiality a part of your group covenant.

How to Use This Leader Guide

Each group will meet for six weeks for the purpose of discussing and putting into practice lessons learned during the week from the Participant Workbook. Your group can tailor the activities and discussion to the time available, usually ranging from 60 to 90 minutes with the majority of that time spent in small group discussion.

The session format described in this guide is designed to aid you as leader and facilitator and to help guide the small group experience. Sessions are easily adaptable for groups that meet for varying lengths of time. Leaders can use the sessions as they are written or choose from among the various components offered, as described below.

Preparing

A brief summary is provided at the beginning of each session so you can begin with an overview and understanding of the main goal of each week's lesson. Knowing the intended goal for the session will enable you to pick questions and manage your time within the small group to be sure the main points are discussed.

Icebreakers and Conversation Starters

Opener options have been included for each session. These activities and conversation starters help your group members connect in a fun, informal manner before entering a time of more personal and reflective sharing. Choose only one activity from the options offered. If your group meets for less than 90 minutes, you may opt to use an opener activity in the first week only, when group members may be meeting for the first time, then forgo openers in the weeks after.

The activities that are included relate in some way to the imagery used in the video or discussion topic, but you are certainly free to select what you think will work best for your group, and you may opt for an alternative opener of your own choosing.

Logistics and Covenant

At your first group meeting, you may want to take time to share important logistical information relevant to your group. This may encompass things such as parking, childcare concerns, start time, discussion format, shared leadership roles, cell phone usage, refreshments, and potential scheduling conflicts.

This is also the time to form and agree on a group covenant: a set of guidelines for behavior in the sessions and mutual promises to respect one another, listen to one another, and treat personal information shared in the group as confidential.

Workbook Review

Encourage group members to bring their Participant Workbooks to each meeting. Each session includes an opportunity for them to share reflections and insights gained from reading the workbook, studying the Scriptures, and writing down their thoughts.

Your group will find that responding to the daily readings and workbook questions will greatly enhance their experience in this study and enrich the group session. Though some group members may not be keeping up in the Participant Workbook, you'll want to include this review portion of the session for those who are doing it. Allowing this time for sharing will not only reinforce those who are practicing this discipline but will also allow others to benefit from other group members' insights and experiences.

Show DVD Video

The DVD includes a 4-5 minute video to "hook" the participants and launch the small group discussion each week. A metaphor is embedded within each video to provide a unique means to consider the specific theme of each session. In addition to the imagery, the video contains an introduction or tie-in to the Scripture passage that will be studied. Finally, each video ends with a question to which group members will share their responses.

Video Discussion

This section provides questions to discuss immediately following the video presentation, to assist group members in considering the imagery, metaphors, and stories used in the video. These questions serve as meaningful segues into the Scripture and Discussion section that will follow.

Scripture and Discussion

This is the most critical and constant component of each session. The session will focus on the Bible passages for that session that are included in the Participant Workbook. Each session will list a Scripture passage to be read aloud and then offer a variety of questions for review, reflection, and personal application.

Note that the sequence and number of questions is up to you and your group, and if desired you may decide to generate your own questions. Those completing the Participant Workbook will have read additional Scriptures during the week, and you are welcome to draw upon those selections to add to the study and discussion of the topic. Whichever questions you decide to use, you are strongly encouraged to include some of the questions with personal-application value that are listed toward the end of each section.

Closing

A closing prayer has been included for each session for those who wish to use it. You may choose to use the prayer listed simply as a resource or not at all. How your prayer is structured and offered is left to the discretion of you and your group. The prayer may be led by you, by another group member, or by the entire group. Sharing of joys and concerns should be included in the closing prayer.

Notes

A section of blank lines is provided at the end of each week's lesson. This space allows you to make notes that will assist you as you lead your small group. It can also be used to insert times, prayer requests, and other relevant information.

Week One

God Loves You

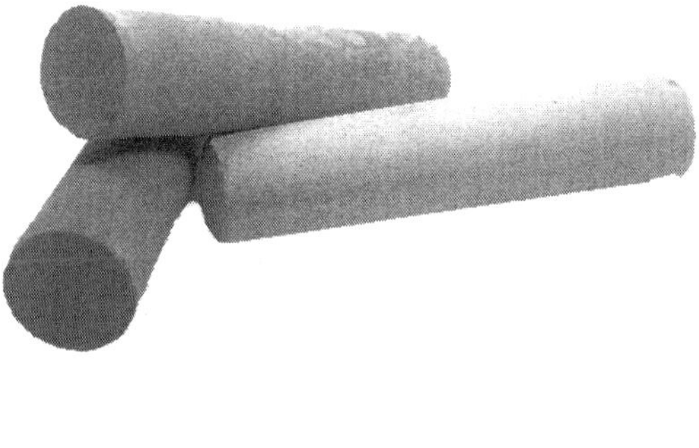

Week One

God Loves You

Preparing

The goal of this week's session is to help participants understand that God loves each of us. We are all God's favorite children. Our self-worth is based on the fact that God loves us and calls us God's children. We are God's children now, not sometime in the distant future. God knows everything about us. God accepts and loves us as we are but refuses to leave us that way. God is with us through every situation, in every trial—protecting, loving, and guiding us. God knows and loves us completely. Since God's character goes into the creation of every person, we know that God's Spirit is ready and willing to work within us. We can have as much respect for ourselves as our Maker has for us.

Consider God's plan to use each of us in our unique circle of friends and relationships to bring others closer to God. What we share with others about God will have the most value when we are willing to share our own life experience and what we know to be true about God. When we come to live by this truth, we will no longer see an imperfect spouse, a cranky neighbor, or an irritating co-worker. Instead we will view everyone we meet as one of God's favorite children.

The Scripture lesson in Day 4 of this week, Luke 15, was selected to focus participants' attention on God's love for God's children. Discussion questions were designed to help participants understand that God's love is based not on what we do for God but on who we are—beloved children made in the divine image. We don't always deserve this love, but God loves us anyway.

Getting Started

As this is the first week of a new study for your group, it is important to allow adequate time for introductions. Even if most of your group members are familiar with one another, using an icebreaker will strengthen connections and will be of great benefit to newcomers. Provide name tags for the group, and consider choosing one of the following activities to help group members get to know one another and to prepare for their time together.

Icebreakers (choose one)

1. **M&M Sharing:** Pass around a bag or bowl of M&Ms and invite group members to help themselves but not eat yet. After the candy has been passed, instruct the group to share one fact about themselves for every piece of candy they took. (Note: Any item can be substituted for M&Ms, such as pennies, popcorn, and other brands of candy.)
2. **Something Few People Know About Me:** Ask members to introduce themselves and share one fact about themselves that is little known. Examples: having nine siblings, being the baby of the family, having hiked to the bottom of the Grand Canyon.
3. **Categorical Descriptors:** Choose a category, such as cars, sports, food, or shoes, and ask each member to name an object within that category that may describe them. Examples: one person might be a pair of spikes because they like to dig deep into things; another might choose a slipper because it offers warmth and comfort; someone else might name fajitas because they are full of zest and spice; another might choose milk because it is wholesome and familiar.
4. **Motion Name Game:** Have the members of your group introduce themselves by saying their names and demonstrating motions to go with them. As each group member offers her or his name, the entire group responds with "Hi, _______," repeating the name and the motion. This continues until all group members have given their names and motions.

Logistics and Covenant

Depending upon whether you are a new or previously formed small group, the amount of time devoted to this portion of the study will vary. "How to Use This Leader Guide" suggests some information that may be appropriate here. Regardless of group history, all groups are encouraged to make a covenant with one another for this six-week study.

Workbook Review

This week's readings focused on gaining a fuller understanding of God's love for each of us. Read aloud 1 John 3:1-3. Share responses to the question from Day 1: "What does it mean to see yourself as a child of God?" Or, in groups of 3-5, share one Scripture or reflection from which you gained new insight into God's love for each of us.

Discussing

SHOW DVD VIDEO

Video Discussion

In the video, Tom Berlin gives an example of a man who lost everything but still had hope for his life because of his faith in God. How hard would it be for you to continue trusting God if you had the same experience?

Why is it so easy for the children in the video to understand that God loves them and so hard for us?

Scripture and Discussion

The Parable of the Lost Son follows two other parables in the Gospel of Luke—the Lost Sheep and the Lost Coin. Jesus uses these three parables to emphasize his point. What do these three stories, told by Jesus, have in common? Ask the group to discuss the Parable of the Lost Son (Luke 15):

1. What do verses 13-16 reveal about the younger brother?
2. What realization does the younger son have in verses 17-20?
3. What does verse 20 reveal about God's love for us?

4. Why do you think the father's view of his son was so different from the son's view of himself?
5. Why is it often hard for people to accept the fact that God loves them?
6. Have you ever felt unworthy to be called a child of God? Why or why not?
7. In what ways do you think God views you differently from the way you view yourself?

Closing

Invite group members to share joys and concerns within the group. When all have shared, close with the following prayer or your own.

Holy, loving, and merciful God, we come before you in awe of your deep, abiding, and unconditional love for us. As we spend time together in your Word, we are overwhelmed by the width and depth of your love.

Thank you that each of us is one of your favorite children. Give us the desire to recognize the opportunities you give us to share this truth with others, and the assurance that you are with us as we do so. As we have been blessed, so may we go forth and be a blessing to others.

In the name of Jesus Christ, your Son. Amen.

Notes

Week Two

God Understands You

Week Two

God Understands You

Preparing

The goal of this week's session is to help participants come to a fuller understanding of God's nearness. Humanity is a work in progress. Through faith, we are being transformed into the people God wants us to be. Christians believe that God came to be our guide. God refused to stay at a distance but instead came as Christ into our world, and as a result we can be assured that God completely understands us. Christ is our guide for the journey. He takes us to the good places we long to go and will never leave us alone.

The imagery of the gardener, vine, and branches in John 15, the Scripture passage for Day 2 of this week, shows that we do not have the power to produce godly characteristics on our own. Just as the branches must be connected to a tree to bear fruit, the believer must be connected to Christ to bear the fruit of the Spirit. According to Galatians 5:22-23, the fruit of the Spirit is love, joy, peace, patience, kindness, goodness, faithfulness, gentleness, and self-control. Christian fruit is produced by the Holy Spirit, not merely by the moral discipline of trying to live a good life. It is the indwelling of the Holy Spirit, Christ in us, that produces Christian virtues in the believer's life.

Getting Started

Choose one of the following icebreakers as an introduction to your small-group time. This will allow members to connect with one another so they can look together at this week's topic.

Icebreakers (choose one)

1. **Draw a Map:** Make a list of various local places you feel most participants in your group are familiar with. Then, in the group, pass out blank pieces of paper and writing instruments. Name each place and ask participants to make a map of how to get there from where you are meeting. Tell them they will have three minutes to do this. At the end of the time, have individuals pair up and present their maps, coupled with verbal directions. Give them two minutes to do this. At the end of the two minutes, ask them to consider the following questions: Did you find it easier to follow a visual map or the verbal directions? Why, even when we are supplied with a map and clear instructions, do we sometimes still get lost?
2. **Conversation Opener:** Have group members pair up and share their worst story about a time they got lost, either walking or driving. Give the pairs 3-5 minutes to share, and then invite everyone to come back together as one group. Ask how it felt to be lost, how they found their way back, and whether in retrospect they understood where they made their mistakes.

Workbook Review

This week's readings focused on coming to a fuller understanding of God's nearness and God's understanding of each of us. God, through Christ, knows the human experience. As a result, we can trust God to understand us and to guide us down a path that leads to a beautiful place.

Share responses to the question from Day 3: "In your own words, write what we learn about Christ in Isaiah 53:11-12."

Discussing

SHOW DVD VIDEO

Video Discussion

Recall Tom Berlin's story about getting lost on the trail. What does the story tell us about searching for God?

Drawing on the imagery of countless leaves, how hard is it for you to grasp the idea that God can know you on an intimate level among all the people of the earth?

Scripture and Discussion

Read aloud John 15:1-17 and discuss the following:

1. What analogy is used in the passage regarding a right relationship with God for living life to the fullest? Who is the gardener? Who is the vine? Who are the branches?
2. What does verse 2 say that the gardener must do to assure healthy plant growth?
3. What do verses 4-8 say is essential for bearing fruit?
4. What necessary action on our part is described in verse 10?
5. What command does Jesus share in verses 12 and 17?
6. In the video, Tom discusses various perspectives we can have regarding our relationship with God. Within the group, share your current perception of God or describe how you view your relationship with God.
7. The imagery of the gardener, vine, and branches is useful in helping us understand God. Like the gardener, God desires an active relationship with us and wants to nurture and grow us into wondrous full bloom. An important point here is that our relationship is based not on what we do for God but on what God does within and through us. Explore this distinction. How does it strengthen or change your understanding of your relationship with God, our Creator?
8. Highlight or take note of the words "remain in me" (verse 4), "love" (verses 9-13), and "bear fruit" (verse 16). Why do you suppose these words are used in the passage, and what is the relationship among them?
9. Visits to the grocery store attest to the fact that fruit varies in quality. What factors contribute to vibrant, healthy "fruit" as described in the passage? What is the condition of the fruit that you are bearing in your life right now? What changes, if any, would you like to make?

Closing

Invite group members to share joys and concerns within the group. When all have shared, close with the following prayer or your own.

Lord Jesus Christ, you are our Savior and Guide. You love each of us and accept us as works in progress. Thank you that we do not need to be lost and can count on you to be our trustworthy and beloved guide. Thank you that, when sin and wrong living ensnare us, you can be trusted to take us where we need to go. Thank you, too, that as we experience transformation in our own lives, you have given us a story that can be shared with others to offer hope and redemption.

Lord God, we have experienced bountiful blessings in our relationship with you. May we truly understand and take to heart that we have been blessed to be a blessing. Guide us through our hesitancies, our inhibitions, and our reluctance to acknowledge you, so that instead we may proclaim with confidence that you, who began a good work in each of us, will be faithful to complete it in the day of Christ Jesus. Hear us as we share these joys and concerns of our group. . . .

In Jesus' holy and precious name we pray. Amen.

Notes

Week Three

God Forgives You

Week Three

God Forgives You

Preparing

The goal of this week's session is to help participants reach a fuller understanding of the forgiving and compassionate nature of God. Romans 7, the Scripture passage for Day 2 of this week, was chosen because it gives participants a solid platform on which to discuss and come to an understanding of our own sinfulness.

Sin is separation from God, and sin is experienced when we live in ways that are contrary to God's will. When we act according to our own will, we often find ourselves feeling isolated from God and the people around us. Repentance is the act of turning to God. We can do this when we begin to trust in God's love for us and to obey God's will for our lives.

Getting Started

Choose one of the following icebreakers as an introduction to your small-group time. This will allow members to connect with one another and to prepare themselves together to examine this week's topic.

Icebreakers (choose one)

1. **Sharing at Length:** Pass around a skein of yarn, a ball of string, or a roll of toilet paper. Instruct group members to cut or tear off whatever amount they choose. After everyone has taken some, direct the group to share what they have learned about God during this study in the following way:

- **String or Yarn:** Talk while wrapping the length of string or yarn around your finger. Keep sharing until all the string or yarn has been used.
- **Toilet Paper:** For each square of toilet paper you took, share something different you have learned about God so far in this study.

2. **My Two Cents' Worth:** Pass around a roll or basket of pennies, instructing everyone to take two. When everyone has their coins, invite the group to share their "two cents' worth" about what they learned during the first two sessions of the study. One penny could be an idea or insight from Week 1, and the second penny could be an idea or insight from Week 2.
3. **Signature Cards:** Pass out index cards to the group. Ask group members to write their names on the cards along with one thing they have learned about God during the study so far. Ask them to spend only a minute or two doing this. At the end of the time, explain that what they just wrote is their "signature comment." Then have everyone pass their cards to the left and add their signature comment to the card they receive. Continue passing the cards to the left until the cards have gone all the way around the group. Encourage participants to keep the card they ended up with as a means of reviewing all they have been learning.

Workbook Review

This week's readings focused on Scripture passages that help us understand that we can experience freedom and forgiveness through Christ and new life in the Spirit. In groups of 3-5, share one Scripture or reflection from which you gained new insight into these experiences.

Read aloud Romans 7:14-25. Share responses to the question from Day 2: "Express in your own words the dilemma Paul describes in verses 14-20. In whom did Paul find the answer to this battle that raged within him?"

Discussing

SHOW DVD VIDEO

Video Discussion

In the video, Tom Berlin says that people unfamiliar with the Christian faith sometimes view Christianity as a set of rules. People want freedom, not a set of rules. As believers, we know that on our own we are not as free as we think and that knowing Christ gives us the freedom we long for. In your experience, how have you found freedom in knowing Christ?

Jesus came to show us a life of righteousness, a life that is fundamentally better than anything we find on our own. Have you experienced the freedom that can be found in Christ? When friends share the frustrations in their own lives, can you say, "You know, there's a reason you are frustrated . . ." and then tell them why?

Scripture and Discussion

Read aloud John 8:1-11 and discuss the following:

1. Who is present in this passage, and why are they there?
2. What is happening in verses 1 & 2? What event happens to change the scene in verse 3?
3. Why do the religious leaders bring the adulterous woman to Jesus and put her on public display?
4. How does Jesus differ from the religious leaders in his attitude toward the woman? Why? How do you imagine his tone of voice, body posture, and interaction with the woman?
5. What is the response of the accusers to Jesus' directive?
6. What does Jesus ask when the crowd has dispersed? What is Jesus' final response to the woman in verse 11?
7. Sin is anything we do that separates us from God or improperly divides us from other people. Why is it important for us to acknowledge our sin?

8. What do we learn from this reading that Christ offers us? Why is his offer critical to understanding Christian faith?
9. Christ's gift of forgiveness can't be given unless we acknowledge our need for it. Similarly, the gift is useless unless it is received. Explain the difference between Christ offering us forgiveness for our sins, and our accepting it.
10. How have you experienced the grace of knowing that you are accepted by Christ no matter what you bring to him?

Closing

Invite group members to share joys and concerns within the group. When all have shared, close with the following prayer or your own.

Lord Jesus Christ, you have offered us complete freedom through your forgiveness of our sins, which was accomplished by your death on the cross. Such a generous and amazing gift is hard for us to fathom, and yet we know we simply must accept it. Forgive our hesitancy to receive what you have offered us so freely. Help us in our doubts, our holding back, and our inability to trust you with our lives.

Thank you for the Scriptures and this discussion time, which have allowed us to hear how lives are changed because of you. May we see your presence in our lives, acknowledge the difference that it makes in our living, and love those around us enough to share what we know about you. We ask that the fruit of your Spirit might grow in our lives so that others truly see Christ in us. Make us ever ready to care and share with those you love, as we pray for these people whose names have been shared. . . .

It is in the name of the One who has extended amazing grace to each of us that we pray. Amen.

Notes

Week Four

God Wants You to Be Free

Week Four

God Wants You to Be Free

Preparing

The goal of this week's session is to help participants come to a fuller understanding of the freedom that comes from choosing Christ. In the letter we know as Colossians, Paul was writing to a local church in the town of Colossae in the first century. The church Paul had started at Ephesus had been fruitful and had eventually started satellite churches; the church in Colossae was apparently one of these. Paul had never visited the church, but he was excited about their faith. In the letter, Paul encouraged them to keep on growing, changing, and living in ways that honored Christ.

Christians believe that choosing Christ shows we are mindful of the place that Jesus takes in our lives. With Christ we choose a life that is full, rich in experience, and productive, in the way that God intended it to be.

Getting Started

This week's session examines free will and our ability to choose. Select one of the following icebreakers to practice choosing and prioritizing.

Icebreakers (choose one)

1. **Dream Trip:** Pair members within your group and have them share with one another the destination of their dream trip. Tell them there are no constraints of finances or time, so they can go wherever they would like.

2. **Desert Island Scenario 1:** Pair group members. Tell them they have just learned they will be stranded on a desert island for one year and will have available to them only three foods for the entire year. Ask each pair to share with one another what the three foods would be and why.

3. **Desert Island Scenario 2:** Pair group members. Tell them they are going to be stranded on a desert island for one year, and they will be allowed to take just one item with them. What would that item be and why?

4. **Farmer Challenge:** Divide the large group into subgroups of 3-5 members each. Give the group the following problem and allow a few minutes for them to come up with a solution:

   A farmer has a dog, a sack of grain, and a live chicken, all of which he must take across a river. The boat will only carry him and one of the things at a time or it will sink. Without the farmer, the dog would kill the chicken; and without the farmer, the chicken would eat the grain. How does the farmer get all three across the river safely?

   Answer: The farmer takes the chicken across and comes back; then he takes the grain and comes back with the chicken; he then takes the dog and comes back; then he takes the chicken.

Workbook Review

This week's readings focused on discovering the joy of being in a right relationship with God and becoming the person God desires us to be by choosing Christ to lead our lives. In groups of 3-5, share a Scripture or reflection from which you gained new insight in your during the week.

All the readings during the week revealed the consistent choice being offered to humankind throughout history: "Choose this day whom you will serve...." Big decisions take careful thought and evaluation. With a partner, share why choosing Christ is such a hard decision for many to make.

Discussing

SHOW DVD VIDEO

Video Discussion

In the video, Tom Berlin likens the relationship God desires with us to our earthly parent-child relationships. God longs for relationship with us, but we often keep our distance from God because we realize we don't have much in common with our Creator. God is all-loving, all-powerful, perfect, and holy. We're not. What role does Jesus play in helping us choose to have a relationship with God?

At the end of the video, Tom says, "My mother once told me that the greatest moment of parenting is the moment when you realize your children have chosen to be your friends. That is the moment God is looking forward to." Explain what you understand this comment to mean. Does it describe your relationship with God?

Scripture and Discussion

Turn to Colossians 1 and discuss the following:

1. What is Paul thankful for in verses 3-5?
2. In verse 6, what does Paul say has been happening?
3. List a few things from verses 10-12 that Paul says will be pleasing to the Lord in every way.
4. In verses 13-14, what does Paul say God has done for us?
5. In verses 21-22, how does Paul say we experience reconciliation?
6. What does Paul say we must do in response to this reconciliation?
7. Share your definition or understanding of the concept of free will as it relates to sin and your relationship with God. Why does God make our relationship with him and our obedience to him a choice rather than a mandate?
8. What do you learn about Christ in this passage? What does it mean to you to live a life "worthy of Christ"?

9. Prioritizing our lives is a daily discipline for Christians. Why? What things draw you toward Christ? What things draw you away?
10. Consider your own life experience concerning a choice for Christ. What evidence do you see in your own life or in the lives of others that choosing Christ is the right decision? Does knowing Christ make enough difference in your life that you believe knowing him will make a difference to others as well?
11. What are some ways you can grow in your knowledge of God's will for your own life?
12. What does Paul describe as hallmarks of a healthy church?
13. What is it about a church or the members of a local congregation that helps others see God?

Closing

Invite group members to share joys and concerns within the group. When all have shared, close with the following prayer or your own.

Lord Jesus Christ, you are the image of the invisible God, the firstborn over all creation. Through you, all things are held together. Through you, we have been reconciled to God. Thank you for the gift of free will so we might experience the fullness of a redeemed relationship with you. Through the power of your Holy Spirit, help us to live a life worthy of Christ, bearing fruit in every good work and sharing the gospel with those who need to hear it. May our lives be a living witness for you. It is with confidence that we share our joys and concerns, knowing that you can be trusted with all things....

In the name of Jesus Christ we pray. Amen.

Notes

Week Five

God Wants You to Change

Week Five

God Wants You to Change

Preparing

The goal of this week's session is to help participants come to a fuller understanding of how the Holy Spirit equips us to live a holy life. Through the power of God's Holy Spirit, we really do have the power to change and become the people God wants us to be. The Holy Spirit works in us to assure us of God's unconditional love and forgiveness, reminding us of what we know about God. The Holy Spirit reveals and convicts us of our sin, equips us for every good work, and helps us resist temptation. The Holy Spirit gives us wisdom, guidance, and direction for living.

This week's Scripture passage for Day 4, 1 Corinthians 2, was selected to focus participants' attention on the gift of the Holy Spirit. It is a good starting point in discussing the contrast between human wisdom and God's wisdom. Wisdom is a highly coveted trait, and Paul was preaching to the people in Corinth that true wisdom requires believers to be guided by the Holy Spirit. Paul wrote in his letter that Jesus was misunderstood and rejected by those whom the world considered wise and great. While no one can comprehend God, we can gain insight into God's plans by having the "mind of Christ." It is through the Holy Spirit that believers can begin to know God's thoughts and find the truth that belongs to all people. The Holy Spirit gives us the strength and courage to make changes in our lives that will lead to a full, rich, and purpose-filled life.

Getting Started

Choose one of the following icebreakers as an introduction to your small-group time. These activities will help group members connect with one another and prepare themselves together to examine this week's topic.

Icebreakers (choose one)

1. **The Most Change:** Divide the large group into subgroups of 4-5 each. Instruct the subgroups that they are to count the total amount of coin change they have together. Remind members to count their own personal change before coming up with a subgroup total so that change can be readily retrieved. The subgroup with the most change wins. Tell the group that in this week's session, they'll be looking at the most "change" that individuals can experience because of the presence and guidance of the Holy Spirit in our lives.

2. **Pair and Share Review:** Place various colored dot stickers on participants' name tags prior to their arrival, or give out stickers in random order as participants arrive. Then, when the activity starts, have participants group with one another by like color. Instruct the group members to each share one important thing they have learned from this study so far, or one opportunity God has provided enabling them to share what they are learning in this study.

Workbook Review

This week's readings focused on coming to a fuller understanding of the Holy Spirit's power to change an individual's life and produce the qualities of Christ in a consistent fashion. In groups of 3-5, share a Scripture or reflection from which you gained new insight this past week.

Read aloud Psalm 51 and share responses to the question from Day 1: "What is David's prayer in verse 10 of today's Scripture? What do you understand a 'steadfast spirit' to mean?"

Discussing

SHOW DVD VIDEO

Video Discussion

Consider the contrast that Tom Berlin makes in the video: "Over hundreds of years, people have changed the world dramatically. Yet, over the same period of time, people have not changed a bit." What issues do we struggle with? Why is there so little evidence of change?

What keeps you from asking for the power of God to change your life?

Scripture and Discussion

Read aloud 1 Corinthians 2 and discuss the following:

1. Where does Paul say he got his power for preaching?
2. By what means does verse 10 say the truth is revealed?
3. What is the contrast in verses 14-15 between a person with the Spirit and a person without?
4. What does the final sentence of verse 16 say the Spirit gives us?
5. Some Bible translations subtitle this passage of Scripture as "Wisdom from the Spirit." Contrast human wisdom and God's wisdom.
6. What value do you place on wisdom? How is it associated with your definition of success?
7. What is significant about Paul's clarity of purpose in his statement in verse 2? How do you align with Paul in your sense of purpose?
8. What does it mean to you to have God's wisdom in your day-to-day living because the Holy Spirit lives within you?
9. How can your responsiveness to the Spirit's promptings and guidance be increased in your life?
10. How would you explain the working of the Holy Spirit in your life? What evidence could you share to validate it as a living presence in your life?

Closing

Invite group members to share joys and concerns within the group. When all have shared, close with the following prayer or your own.

Most Holy and Loving God, you long for the best for each of us. Your desire is for each of us to know you and to live life abundantly. So strong is your desire that you have equipped us with the indwelling presence and power of your Holy Spirit. Thank you, God, for loving us so much, for knowing us so fully, and for providing for us beyond what we can imagine.

We are grateful that because of your Spirit, real change is possible for each of us. We praise you for the freedom that comes in knowing you. We rejoice that each of us truly is a new creation. The old has gone, the new has come. Let us not keep this good news to ourselves, God, but instead, through the prodding and provision of your Holy Spirit, make us ever willing to share what we know to be true. We share with you now the concerns of our hearts....

As we leave this place, open our eyes to see the opportunities you place before us and make us ever willing to be ambassadors for the One who gave his life on our behalf, our Lord and Savior Jesus Christ. Amen.

Notes

Week Six

God Wants to Be With You Forever

Week Six

God Wants to Be With You Forever

Preparing

The goal of this week's session is to help participants come to a fuller understanding of the kingdom of heaven. God's desire is that we spend eternity with him, that we choose to be with the one we love forever.

In the video, Tom Berlin suggests that heaven is really the eternal continuation of the choices we make on earth. In previous sessions throughout this study, we learned that God is a loving God and values our free-will choice. A loving God who honors our choices is not going to make us spend eternity with our Creator if we did not choose that relationship in our earthly life. The Scripture chosen for Day 2 of this week, Luke 14:15-24, shows us people who were late or had excuses and so lost their places at the banquet. The story for them must have ended with great regret.

Sharing with others what we know about God is not manipulating others into agreeing with our personal beliefs. Rather it is being willing to be honest about our own life and faith experiences that reveal simple truths about God.

Getting Started

Since this is the final week of the six-week study, take time for participants to engage in one of the review activities below. Remind group members that they may forget many details about the study, but recalling and naming the Six Things We Should Know About God will be of great use to them in sharing the experience of God with others.

Review Activity (choose one)

1. **Memorable Presentation:** Depending on the size of your group, divide participants so there are six groups of equal number. Give each group a paper with one of the Six Things everyone should know about God written on it. Give the groups 5-10 minutes to develop a memorable presentation of that truth about God. Presentations might, for example, be in the form of a song, limerick, rap, commercial, news interview, or poster. If the group is too small to divide into six subgroups, pick one of the six things for the whole group to present.

2. **Window Paning:** Using chart-size paper or posterboard, draw a six-square grid. Ask participants to recall what five things they learned during the past five weeks that everyone should know about God. (The five things are: God Loves You, God Understands You, God Forgives You, God Wants You to Be Free, and God Wants You to Change.) Write each statement in one of the first five grids. As you do, assign a picture symbol to the statement. (For God Loves You, for example, the group might draw a heart; for God Understands You, the group might draw a mirror; and so on.) After the five squares have been completed, give the group the sixth statement: God Wants to Be With You Forever. Ask them to put the statement in the sixth square, along with a picture symbol. When all the squares are filled in, practice saying the six things aloud together as a group. Do this in sequential order at first, and then by random pointing. Cover the words, and see if the group can name the six things by picture symbols only.

Workbook Review

This week's readings focused on coming to a fuller understanding of the kingdom of heaven and what Jesus taught about this topic. In groups of 3-5, share a Scripture or reflection from which you gained insight into this understanding during the week.

Read aloud John 3 as a group and share responses to the question from Day 4: "Nicodemus was obviously an intelligent man. Why do you suppose it was so hard for him to understand what Jesus was saying?"

Discussing

SHOW DVD VIDEO

Video Discussion

In the video, Tom Berlin talks about various views people hold about how one "gets into heaven." What is your understanding of heaven and how a person gets there? Do good works play a part in this? Why or why not?

Jesus uses the wedding banquet as his image of heaven. It is a great image: family, friends, food, drink, and celebration. God has offered us an invitation to the banquet. The question is, how will you reply to that invitation, and who are some people you'd like to invite to the party?

Scripture and Discussion

Read aloud Luke 14:15-24 and discuss the following:

1. What does verse 18 say about how invitees responded to the invitation?
2. List the excuses offered for not attending the banquet:

   a. ____.

   b. ____.

   c. ____

3. How does the master respond when those he invited make excuses and do not attend?
4. What is the master's desire for his house in verse 23?
5. Why do you suppose so many people, like those invited to the banquet, say no to God's invitation?
6. What did the video and readings this week suggest is the possible risk of making excuses or saying no to God's invitation?
7. Choosing Christ is a big decision. Some may not be motivated to choose by the promise of eternal existence with God, which may seem too remote or speculative. For those who believe, what difference in life on this side of heaven does choosing Christ make?

8. Throughout the Scriptures this week, we read of God's desire to spend eternity with his children. If that is God's desire, why don't all people automatically dwell in heaven with God?
9. How has your study of Jesus' teaching on the kingdom of heaven affected your view of others who do not know Christ or who have not yet made the choice to follow Christ?

Closing

Take a moment to pose the following questions to your group before praying: What is your hope about yourself as you close the pages of this study? What do you hope to retain and put into practice?

Invite group members to share joys and concerns with the group. When all have shared, close with the following prayer or your own.

Holy and most merciful God, how great you are to send your one and only Son, Jesus Christ, to die for our sins and redeem us unto you. In response to this great gift, may each of us, through the help of your Holy Spirit, choose to make you the first priority in our lives so that we might know the fullness of life on both sides of heaven.

Give us the heart of Christ, filled with compassion for those who have yet to know you. Allow them, through our words and deeds, to see the difference you make in our lives so they too might have abundant life. Specifically, we pray today for … and we share other concerns for those we love….

Lord Jesus Christ, as we leave this place, may we truly be your ambassadors, equipped for every good work and motivated by your love and teaching to go into all the world and make disciples of all nations. It is in your holy, forgiving, and magnificent name we pray. Amen.

Notes

Notes

Notes

28357524R00036

Made in the USA
Middletown, DE
11 January 2016